MIRROR WORK
WORKS

MIRROR WORK WORKS

21-Day Self-Love Experience

Greta Counts

Mountain Arbor
Press
Alpharetta, GA

ISBN: 978-1-6653-0395-8 - Paperback
eISBN: 978-1-6653-0396-5 - ePub

052722

☉This paper meets the requirements of ANSI/NISO Z39.48-1992 (Permanence of Paper)

Edited by: Sharman J. Monroe, www.sharmansedits.com

I dedicate this book to my cousin, Lisa. Gone but not forgotten. I love you always and forever.

And to everyone reading this book, remember to love yourself unconditionally, because you are beautiful and worthy of love. For to love ourselves is to remember that we don't have to do anything to experience the love that we are. Today and every day, I grant you permission to awaken to the truth of who you really are. Be still and know that you are love.

21-Day Self-Love
Mirror Work Experience

Preface

The Mirror Work technique is a wonderful power tool that you can use to change how you see yourself and create a more loving relationship with yourself and others.

Mirror Work lifts the veils of illusion about your unworthiness, feelings of insecurity, inferiority, and inadequacy. It diminishes the imposter syndrome and reveals the love within.

Ultimately, you will see yourself through loving eyes and begin to practice unconditional self-love, self-acceptance, and self-compassion. This process will open you to be more receptive to love, and you will find it easier to love and accept others unconditionally.

We are spiritual beings having a human experience. And this book offers you a tangible way to engage with yourself physically and spiritually, as well as mentally and emotionally. It offers a holistic approach to building a loving relationship with the most important person you will ever meet...YOU. Inner healing counts. Let's heal your life.

As a transformational coach, I have observed the power that loving yourself can have on your relationships with life and others. I have watched its positive effect in the lives of my clients, and I have certainly experienced it myself. What I know for sure is that the power of self-love is powerful!

Looking as far back as 1998, it is clear to me that my discipline and commitment to the daily practice of Mirror Work has and continues to transform my life exponentially. I became more self-aware, and I learned to love the unlovable parts of myself. Without realizing it, I became my own best friend. Building an up-close and personal relationship with myself using Mirror Work has not only improved my relationship with me, but it has also enhanced my relationship with God and others. I have written this book in hopes that you, too, will enjoy the benefits it brings.

Acknowledgments

To my mother, you are so beautiful, brilliant, loving, courageous, and wise; a woman of integrity, a woman of God who modeled excellence for me to follow in heart, mind, and deed. Thank you.

To my beautiful twin daughters, Chelsea & Chela, you are an answered prayer. You are my special gift from God. From the day you were born, you were both my mirrors, always reflecting back to me areas of opportunity for me to be more, to change myself for the better. I love you both always. Thank you.

To all my beloved clients now and over the years, you are all my true heroes, and I am deeply grateful for allowing me to be a part of your healing journey. Thank you for sharing your lives, your stories, your pains, and your victories with me.

To Mary Kay Ash, who launched a business with the purpose of empowering women. During my seven years as an Independent Sales Director with Mary Kay, Inc., I unknowingly used the mirror technique every single day. My devotion to being a top-performing leader required me to do my inner work, and I watched myself become a woman of strength, courage, and wisdom using this daily practice of self-love. The philosophy of God first, family second, and career third helped me prioritize myself and my life in ways that would prove to be life-changing for me as a woman and a mother. Thank you.

To Dr. Patricia Crane, founder and CEO of Heart Inspired Presentations, LLC., the work we did to become licensed Heal Your Life© workshop facilitators and coaches based on the philosophy of Louise Hay included mirror work. The requirement to use the mirror technique became a part of my daily spiritual practice again and continues to transform my life and the lives of my clients. Thank you.

To my wonderful editor, Sharman Monroe, you are a godsend. You were patient, gentle, loving, and kind during this process. I appreciate you. Thank you.

What's In It For Me?

You may be asking yourself, *Why am I doing this?* Let me help you know why.

You can expect to shift from:

Hurting	=>	Healing
Isolation	=>	Intimacy
Blame	=>	Self-Responsibility
Self-Rejection	=>	Self-Acceptance
Self-Abandon	=>	Self-Parenting
Powerlessness	=>	Empowerment
Self-Discovery	=>	Self-Discipline
Self-Hatred	=>	Self-Love

You can expect to gain awareness & self-awareness through accountability and application.

You can expect to cultivate a new relationship with yourself, God and others.

Introduction

Welcome to the 21-Day Self-Love Mirror Work Experience!

I am a great advocate of Mirror Work. I have been using the mirror technique since 1998. I became familiar with it during my years as a top-selling Independent Sales Director with Mary Kay, Inc. Standing in front of the mirror became a daily practice for me and was the way I developed the inner confidence to become a direct-selling master and master recruiter. During my seven years there, I said affirmations in the mirror daily to manifest unbridled success, including the use of four free cars, three of which were the signature pink Cadillac.

Mirror Technique

In 2012, I received my certification as a Certified Heal Your Life ® Workshop Facilitator and Licensed Heal Your Life ® Coach and learned that the mirror work technique was popularized by Louise Hay in her best-selling book, *You Can Heal Your Life.* In it, she asserts that the mirror technique is a wonderful way to shift your consciousness. If you have used the mirror work technique before now, then this is an opportunity for deeper healing.

What is Mirror Work?

Simply put, Mirror Work is a self-help method to increase your ability to practice self-love. Mirror Work is a daily spiritual practice of looking into your own eyes and expressing the growing sense of love you have for yourself. It is giving yourself the gift of your own undivided attention. It is looking inward to explore, uncover and discover the beauty and love within.

It is written, "I and the Father are One." I believe Mirror Work is the opportunity to communicate with the indwelling presence of God within you.

How does it work?

Mirror Work means looking into your eyes in the mirror and saying positive things to yourself such as, "I love you," or "You are doing the best you can," or "You deserve to have a wonderful life," and "I support you."

I highly recommend doing Mirror Work at the beginning of each day. As you progress along this self-love journey, you will be encouraged to use it throughout your entire day.

I also recommend you say the affirmations provided out loud, with feeling at least twice a day; three times is a charm. An affirmation is a personal, positive, present-tense statement used to change something you want to be different or to create something new in your life. Affirmations are a spiritual tool to help you amend your behavior.

This process is divinely designed to awaken you to the love and the loving presence of the Divine within you. You are developing and cultivating an unconditional loving relationship with the most important person you will ever know—You. You will form new habits and increase your self-belief, self-trust and self-compassion.

- You will need a journal, pen, handheld mirror, full-length mirror, tissues and a childhood photo
- Take it personally. This is a journey inward and it is all about you; please do take it personally because it is personal
- I give you permission to love yourself fully

- Please don't distract yourself with mobile devices

Why does it work?

The daily repetition of looking into your own eyes, the window to your soul, helps you cultivate compassion, respect and love for yourself. You develop a more positive self-image, which makes it easier and easier to honor yourself.

This kind of self-discovery offers individual spiritual revelation. This process is not merely metaphysics, a philosophical, abstract theory with no basis in reality; it goes beyond that. It sparks a personal and interior connection with the Divine Presence within.

What are the benefits?

The Mirror Work technique provides infinite benefits. It is the most effective way to help you amend your behavior. Here are a few of those benefits:

- Become your own best friend
- Increase your inner confidence
- Recognize self-value

- Build self-esteem and self-worth
- Develop a stronger connection with God

What can I expect?

- Expect to feel uncomfortable. It is common to look away or to cry as your insecurities rise to the surface.
- Expect to feel silly in the beginning. You may feel like this is unintelligent and doesn't make any sense.
- Expect to hear the volume of your inner critic get louder and louder.
- Expect thoughts to flood your mind, kind and unkind, at a rapid pace.
- Expect to overcome emotional wounds.
- Expect to experience inner healing of mind, spirit and emotions.
- Expect to release the pain, misery and suffering in your life that are the result of a lack of self-love.

Each day, there will be an energizing focus of the day, affirmations to say and additional instructions to help facilitate your inner healing journey.

Action Required

There is an old saying, "You can lead a horse to water, but you can't make her drink." And the same is true with the Self-Love Mirror Work Experience. It works if you work it. You are with yourself 100% of the time and everywhere you go there you are. On this Self-Love journey, you have the opportunity to actively take inventory and amend yourself—your thoughts, your beliefs, your behavior, your attitude, your perspective. If you truly desire to experience more love in your own life, then it must begin with you. I invite you to say it with me now, "Let love begin within me."

Your view of reality is yours and yours alone and your view of yourself is yours as well. The Mirror Work Experience helps you see what you need to see in a gentle way. Feel, go through, allow things to happen, allow it to take its course. During your Mirror Work Experience, the affirmative words you speak about yourself may not feel true initially, but open your mind and your mouth, stick with it and notice the positive changes that happen.

Inner Healing Counts

The Self-Love Mirror Work Experience is a renewal process that opens you to healing from within. You get to take care of yourself in a gentle way.

There is no instant gratification. It takes as long as it takes. So, please be patient with yourself. This is a daily journey, not an overnight event. Healing takes time and is a process. The same is true about Mirror Work. As you journey within, please know that we are in this together. You have my support and my permission to change and let go. The way out is the way through. Take what you need and leave the rest. You have my permission to be fearless and free. You have my permission to take care of yourself, to love yourself and to love yourself first. And whenever clarity is not available, be patient and let it come. Easy does it.

Let the journey of self-discovery and inner healing begin.

WEEK ONE

Day One
THE GIFT OF YOUR OWN ATTENTION

Happy Self-Love Day! Welcome to Day 1 of the 21-Day Self-Love Mirror Work Experience. The energizing focus of the day is THE GIFT OF YOUR OWN ATTENTION. This means to pay attention to yourself and what is happening within you, the thoughts you are having and how you feel inside.

It has been said that the eyes are the windows to the soul. Your eyes gazing into your mirror gives you insight, sensitivity and clarity.

The mirror reflects to you what is going on in the silence of your soul, the silence within you.

Today is a great opportunity to journey within and face yourself and to listen within to what your small still voice is saying. Starting today,

3

make your mirror your friend and take the steps to become your own best friend.

Mirror work takes daily practice and it takes time, but the more you do it, the more comfortable you'll feel. You may even begin to cry, but that's expected and it's okay. In sitting with yourself in this way, you will begin to find out who you really are.

Real change doesn't happen overnight. Giving yourself positive messages during your daily mirror work practice will help you build self-esteem, self-worth, self-compassion, self-acceptance and self-love. You will be motivated to treat yourself more lovingly than ever before. It is imperative that you love yourself and accept yourself before anyone else can.

Remember, the more that you assure yourself that you love and accept yourself, the sooner you will create more joyful experiences in every area of your life. It is the most effective way to make your dreams come true.

Today's exercise is about you being with you, the opportunity to be with yourself—to be still and to be quiet. My first time with mirror work was not easy. I felt uncomfortable looking into my own eyes. Although it may be challenging, I encourage you to do your best.

Growth Work Exercise

Take several slow, deep, cleansing breaths, then pick up your hand mirror. Holding your hand mirror, look into your eyes. Sit with yourself in silence for at least three to five minutes without saying a word. If you are familiar with the mirror technique, please sit for ten to thirteen minutes. Notice the thoughts that pop into your mind. Notice the feelings that accompany those thoughts. Continue breathing slowly, naturally. Focus on what is good about the person you are looking at.

As you gaze into your mirror, think the following thoughts within your mind:

> I am willing to love you exactly as you are.
> I am willing to accept you exactly the way you are.
> I appreciate you for who you are and I thank you for having the courage to begin your journey within.
> I look forward to learning who you are.
> I look forward to loving you more.
> Thank you.

You may want to use your journal to write the thoughts that show up during this exercise and throughout the day. Notice what you notice. No need to judge it; just notice it.

Thank you. Good work. See you tomorrow.

Day Two
GRATITUDE

Happy Self-Love Day! Welcome to Day 2 of the 21-Day Self-Love Mirror Work Experience. The energizing focus of the day is GRATITUDE. An attitude of gratitude changes life for the better. Having an attitude of gratitude, I am reminded that everything in my personal experience is always happening for my highest and best good. It elevates you to a higher state of consciousness. Always and often give thanks.

There are many stressors in life that can make it so easy to be negative, complain or have a pity- party for yourself. The problem is that when this happens, you get more of the same. Gratitude immediately shifts your focus, your energy and your outcomes.

Gratitude is a state of mind and attitude is key. Attitude is your mental approach to life. It is your disposition toward yourself, other people and things.

A grateful attitude helps you to have a spirit of optimism to expect the best and to believe that good comes out of everything. All in all, gratitude is a happy, loving, believing approach that begins within yourself.

One of my favorite demonstrations of the power of gratitude was the story in the Bible when, just *before* Jesus commanded Lazarus to rise, Jesus thanked God for always hearing Him. He didn't wait to express sincere gratitude; He did it in advance. Gratitude makes good out of any and all situations.

Cultivating gratitude will boost your well-being. Whenever something happens in my life, I go to gratitude first. No matter what it is. I have noticed that it shifts my vibration and I immediately experience inner peace. In a state of peace, I am able to console myself from within and then I have clarity about whatever has happened, which reveals to me all that I need to know regarding the situation. I can hear my inner wisdom helping me to have an understanding of what has happened.

When you practice conscious gratitude, you increase your mental, emotional and physical health. Studies show that weekly written records of gratitude can improve health. A daily gratitude journal can help you become more mindful of all the good you have to celebrate in your life and when you focus on the good, you experience more good. Where your attention goes, your energy flows. What you focus on grows and expands. Therefore, it is wise to actively practice gratitude. When you do, you will have more to be grateful for.

When all hell breaks loose, examine your attitude and practice gratitude. Take a moment and give sincere thanks *before* things work out. Be willing to interrogate yourself. Ask yourself, "What attitude am I meeting life with today or in this moment?" Let's take a closer look at your attitude of gratitude today.

Growth Work Exercise

Breathe in through your nose slowly to the count of four, hold your breath to the count of four, then exhale slowly through your mouth to the count of four. Do this at least three times. Go ahead and grab your mirror. Continue breathing slowly, naturally. Now, smile at the person you see gazing back at you in your mirror. Looking into your eyes, say the following out loud, *"With gratitude I have the power, the wisdom and the ability to alter my circumstances for good. In this moment, I am most grateful for _____."* (fill in the blank). Notice the first thing that pops into your mind. Repeat that sentence filling in the blank until you have nothing else to say. You can also complete the sentence: "I am most grateful about _____," or "I am most grateful that _____."

We all have so much to be grateful for. And when we express gratitude, we become appreciative, happy, energetic and joyful. Today, make a commitment with yourself to list in your journal or notes on your mobile device at least twenty-five reasons you are grateful throughout the day. Here's a fun exercise you might enjoy: using the same sentences above, schedule a designated time at the beginning, middle or end of each day and list ten different gratitude statements each time the alarm chimes. Grab your mirror and give thanks:

> I am thankful for today.
> I am grateful for my healthy mind and body.
> I am especially grateful for the opportunity to build a more loving relationship with myself.
> I am grateful that I am using Mirror Work to increase my ability to love others by learning to love me first.
> I am grateful that I have so many wonderful people, experiences and opportunities to be thankful for.

I am grateful for success in all areas of my life.

I am grateful to know that my daily mirror work now opens me to feel more love.

I am grateful for all that is now manifesting in my life.

I am grateful to know that good returns to me multiplied abundantly.

And so it is.

Thank you. Good work. See you tomorrow.

Day Three
ACCEPTANCE

Happy Self-Love Day! Welcome to Day 3 of the 21-Day Self-Love Mirror Work Experience. The energizing focus of the day is ACCEPTANCE.

Many have been offended and hurt by rejection. We have allowed rejection to hurt us because we may not understand that we are the ones that need to accept ourselves, whether others do or not. Rejection is really a gift wrapped in an ugly package that is life's way of redirecting us to the love inside ourselves. So many times, we misuse our energy to feel hurt by rejection from others instead of seeing it as a reminder to look within and practice self-acceptance. Always remember, whenever someone doesn't recognize your good, it doesn't mean that you are not good. It means they don't have the capacity to see and experience your good. So, keep it moving.

Many of our problems stem from self-rejection

and self-hatred of one degree or another. Anytime we feel rejected, we have already subconsciously rejected ourselves. I am reminded of the time my ex-husband and I first got married. My mother-in-law made it clear that my pedigree was not a match for her son or their family. She frequently reminded me that I did not measure up in her eyes. As the matriarch of her family, she would say that she nor the family would ever accept me. And, although it hurt deeply at the time, it redirected me to take an inner look.

A series of anxiety attacks quickly directed me inward. I became introspective and had the realization that, because I was familiar with rejection in my own family experience, I was already practicing self-rejection before I ever met her. She merely magnified what was already inside of me. She only represented an opportunity for me to heal it. And that is exactly what I chose to do.

Today, I am most grateful for that experience because it became a defining moment for me. It redirected me to practice self-acceptance and helped me to learn to heal my own life. Interestingly enough, once I healed myself, our relationship changed for the better. As one of my favorite philosophers, Dr. Ernest Holmes, so eloquently puts it, "Life is a mirror and will reflect back to the thinker what he thinks into it." My mother-in-law was mirroring back to me what was already inside of me.

Have you ever felt the need to be perfect or to do things perfectly? Perfectionism causes us to demand too much from ourselves and is another motivator when seeking acceptance from others. Many of you may be unaware of the long mental lists of things you believe you must do before you can accept yourself. You may think you have to lose weight, go back to school, get a new job, a new relationship, more money, etc. The social circles we belong to help us to believe that we are unacceptable. They add to the many reasons why we think we can't accept ourselves. And even when we finally accomplish those things on the lists, we still find it hard to accept ourselves. Instead, we make a new list of reasons why we can't accept ourselves yet. We will experience acceptance to the degree that we are willing to do it for ourselves first.

It can be so easy to reject yourself by trying to be someone who you think you need to be so you're accepted by others. It takes time, a lifetime to discover who you are, and self-acceptance along the way is paramount. The 21-Day Self-Love experience is a perfect opportunity to point you inward to discover the wonderful person you already are.

Simply put, loving ourselves is nothing more than

accepting ourselves exactly as we are in every moment.

Growth Work Exercise

Grab your hand mirror. Gaze into your eyes. Take at least five slow, deep, cleansing breaths, breathing in through your nose and exhaling gently and ever so slowly through your mouth. Then repeat the following affirmations out loud at least ten times. Please take your time:

> Each rejection in my life experiences lights my way to self-acceptance.
> I am worthy of love and acceptance as I am in this moment.
> I am willing to accept that I am enough.
> I am willing to accept that I deserve good.
> I am willing to accept that I am loved, loving and loveable.
> I am willing to accept that I have everything I need to create a life of love.

Thank you. Good work. See you tomorrow.

Day Four
APPRECIATION

Happy Self-Love Day! Welcome to the Day 4 of the 21-Day Self-Love Mirror Work Experience. The energizing focus of the day is APPRECIATION.

Appreciation is recognition and enjoyment of the good qualities of someone or something. When you feel appreciation, there is vibrational harmony with what you are experiencing at the moment. You feel the true alignment with all that you are and all that is.

In accounting terms, appreciation means "of more value." It is an increase in the value of an asset over time. In finance, there is a formula for calculating appreciation. Here is my simple formula for calculating appreciation emotionally in your life experience:

Appreciate the world around you. Take a few moments each day to notice useful or beautiful things everywhere you go and smile at them.

Express your appreciation of the world to others

every chance you get. Practice appreciating yourself. Express appreciation to others.

The beauty of appreciation is that you are in complete control of how much and how often you engage with it. The key is to amplify it when you feel it. When you feel appreciation, focus on it longer to savor it more and to create more momentum. Since you can choose which direction you point your thoughts and feelings, then you can determine how big they get, how long they last and how often you return to them. Make a commitment to increase your awareness of appreciation in your life. It sustains you when you understand the impulse you are feeling. And when you do, a rendezvous is happening. Appreciation of all that is around you increases your ability to appreciate even more. In other words, you can find your own joy and expand on that joy.

One of the most progressive, productive, effective and easiest things you can ever do is to appreciate everyone and everything that you see. There is always something to appreciate. Appreciation of everything, everywhere, builds a higher momentum of alignment with the Creator.

When you show value for what is around you, you will feel value from within. And this value and appreciation you feel are proportionate with the value and appreciation you express. This feeling of reciprocity is what you have been longing for and it's in your control.

It is so easy to reach for the emotion of appreciation. There is so much around us to appreciate. In this moment, I appreciate our wonderful planet that spins in orbit, the sun that rises and sets each day, the sweet fragrance of the magnolia tree outside my home, the song of the birds, the beauty of the flowers and the sound of the rain. I appreciate the still of the night, the bright moonlight and the cool breeze in the morning. I could go on and on.

By its very definition, appreciation perpetuates more. When we make a conscious decision to reach for the emotion of appreciation as often as we can, we will be filled and receive more appreciation within. There is no price to pay. It is one of the easiest things we could ever do and it is one of the most effective things we can do. There are no words to describe the fulfillment that can be felt from appreciating others and all.

I believe that appreciation expressed is essentially me having worked myself into a place where God is looking through me at someone or something.

The Self-Love Mirror Work Experience is all about you learning to practice self-love, so give your attention to you. Your ability to appreciate yourself means you value yourself, your gifts, talents and abilities, and the value you add to life. Have you ever noticed that when you appreciate yourself, you have a great appreciation for others as well?

When you appreciate yourself and others, it removes judgment and criticism, and releases love. It can be so easy to find fault with others. However, this is minimized when you practice appreciation. Make it your business to catch someone doing good and doing right today. When you focus on their goodness, you experience goodness as well. When you look forward to appreciating someone or something, you expect to accept it unconditionally.

Practice self-appreciation. I encourage you to look for opportunities to appreciate yourself. Notice how many things you do today that deserve your verbal appreciation. Create a running list in your journal. Tell yourself that you appreciate what a great mother, father, friend, business owner, employee, sister, brother, neighbor, colleague, etc., you are. Go deep and explain why you appreciate that quality about yourself. Why does that have so much meaning to you and for you? Because doing this exercise will help you see how much there is to appreciate about you.

Growth Work Exercise

Please close your eyes, breathe in deeply, slowly, gently through your nose to the count of four, hold it for a count of four. Now exhale slowly to the count of four. Do this for three to five minutes. Grab your mirror. Continue breathing naturally, slowly and gently as you repeat the following. Recite these affirmations at least ten times:

> I am willing to appreciate myself exactly as I am.
> I appreciate you exactly as you are.
> There is so much to appreciate about you.
> I appreciate all the wonderful qualities you have.
> You are valuable and I appreciate you.
> Thank you for being you.

Thank you. Good work. See you tomorrow.

Day Five
APPROVAL

Happy Self-Love Day! Welcome to Day 5 of the 21-Day Self-Love Mirror Work Experience. The energizing focus of the day is APPROVAL.

From a very tender age, we are conditioned to seek the approval of others. Our parents, teachers, family and friends praise us when we do what is acceptable in society and shun us when we don't. We get rewarded for doing "good." When we make our parents and friends proud of us, it grooms us to become what I call "approval whores or junkies." We pimp ourselves to the highest bidder for the feeling of approval. And even though it can give us the incentive to be the best we can be, all too often, we do it at the expense of sacrificing our authentic self. We trade our essential selves in for our social self who is most interested in pleasing others. Approval whores are liked and adored by many and often have degrees, status, money and other tangible items that suggest they have received approval. However, they may not even recognize their struggle to approve of themselves. In fact, they may not even know what they like or who they are because they are a cocktail of what others want them to be.

I remember being twenty-six years of age and wondering whose life I was living. I had always been a "Jill-of-all-trades" capable of doing many things well and being all things to many people. I was reading a book called *I Could Do Anything If I Only Knew What It Was* by Barbara Sher and I was having difficulty answering the questions. I was living in Brooklyn, New York at the time and I went home to Atlanta to visit my family and friends. During my visit, I had an epiphany because everyone important to me seemed disappointed in me in some way since I was not meeting their individual expectations of me. At that moment, I was a wife, mother, daughter, niece, best friend, cousin and, with everyone in one room, I wasn't sure which me to be. Based on the comments being made to me, I realized that I had become what I call an "approval whore."

Approval whores say yes to others when they want to say no. They are compliant because they want to feel needed and loved. An approval whore will do what is necessary to meet the expectations of the highest bidder. In other words, for the feeling of approval with the greatest return, a person jumps through hoops, climbs mountains, swims the deep blue sea, all for the approval of that person, church, organization, company, society, sorority, fraternity, etc. Many times, when this happens, we are unaware. Our only noticeable indicator is the diminishing returns of the approval from those who have rendered it and the exhaustion we feel from being inauthentic.

I was completely unaware that I had lived a life of people-pleasing until that moment in time when it all converged. Little did I know I had been making the opinion of others a power greater than myself. The expectations others had of me to meet their approval was not possible unless I continued to forsake myself. I could not be my mother's daughter, my husband's wife, my daughters' mother, my mother-in-law's daughter-in-law, my best friend's bestie based on everyone else's expectation of me.

In Atlanta, I had been a single, career-driven woman with a lot of time on my hands. Then life kicked into high gear when I relocated to Brooklyn, New York. As a wife, mother of twin daughters in the fast-paced entertainment industry, my new life required I have a clear, strong understanding of who I was at all times.

I had lost myself and my identity, trying to be what others wanted me to be. I had to quickly figure out who I was and who I wanted to become and be *that* person and everyone else would just have to take a hike. From that moment of awakening, I have dedicated my life to being my authentic self and that is a full-time job. Today, I often check in with myself by looking in the mirror and asking myself, *Have I self-abandoned?* Mirror Work reminds me that I am a priority and to be true to myself.

Did you know that when you practice self-approval, it opens you to accept others exactly as they are? You learn that in the same way you are okay, so are they. You no longer feel the need or desire to control others, nor do you need them to be who you think they should be. Instead, your attention is on you and being the best you that you can be based on who you want to be.

Who you are is ever-changing because we are all evolving. When you are in tune with yourself through self-approval, you can adapt to change more quickly. But when you are being someone other than yourself, change is harder because you hold on to the person you think you should be based on what others think you should be. That disposition is not sustainable and creates unhappiness and inner turmoil that, in turn, creates stress and strain in your life.

Thankfully, I no longer aimlessly seek the approval of others before my own approval. To put it mildly, "Frankly, my dear, I don't give a damn" about someone else's approval of me. I consciously practice self-approval at all times. I am the one who gets to decide who I am and no one else is qualified to make that decision for me but me. Wayne Dyer says it this way, "I am independent of the good opinion of others."

Growth Work Exercise

Let's begin with our breathwork. Breathe in slowly through your nose and out through your mouth three to five times. Take your time. I invite you to grab your mirror. Take a deep look into the eyes of the best friend you will ever have. The person you are looking at is your forever friend. This person came to share this life experience with you and will be with you to the end.

Breathing gently and slowly repeat these words:

> You are a precious child of the universe.
> There is no one quite like you.
> I approve of you exactly as you are right now.
> You are special. You are unique. You are enough.

You are the only you like you and I love you just the way you are.

I give you permission to be all of who you are.

The world is a better place because of you.

Thank you for being you.

Thank you. Good work. See you tomorrow.

Day Six
PRAISE

Happy Self-Love Day! Welcome to Day 6 of the 21-Day Self-Love Mirror Work Experience. The energizing focus of the day is PRAISE.

Praise is defined as the expression of approval or admiration for someone or something. Praise is a state of mind. Praise builds up the inner spirit; criticism breaks it down. We need to praise ourselves a lot and quiet the inner critic.

Make praise a habit. Praise the good qualities in yourself and in others. Discipline yourself to praise God, praise good and praise yourself on a regular basis. When you praise yourself, it builds character, confidence and esteem.

The power of praise affects everything in your life. Everything responds to praise. There is a direct correspondence to praise. Praise a child for the good he or she does and it motivates the child to be better.

The same is true for a pet. Conversely, when you criticize them, it demoralizes them and breaks their spirit. For those who have been told they will never amount to anything, it can take a lifetime of effort to create success.

Maybe you grew up in a home where negative words and criticism were normal. Now that you are an adult, you have the power to change the words you say to yourself. Raise your spirits, raise your experiences with the discipline of self-praise. Starting today, say only good things about yourself to yourself and to others. Make a decision to no longer put yourself down or dismiss yourself in any way. You matter and how you feel about yourself matters. Words have power. Use your words to praise.

I once read about an agricultural experiment conducted years ago. Every day a group of agriculturalists would stand around Plot A. They would praise that plot of corn as it began to grow, saying good things about it. They would tell it how wonderful and beautiful it was. Then they would go to Plot B and bad-mouth it. And the two plots of corn corresponded to the praise and the criticism that was lavished upon it. Plot A grew and multiplied; it was fruitful. Plot B was stunted, scrawny and unfruitful and didn't amount to anything. This experiment is a testament to the power of praise and the power of our words.

Growth Work Exercise

It's time to grab your mirror. Gazing into your eyes, breathe deeply. Slowly inhale and exhale for several minutes. When you feel still and calm inside, repeat the following words out loud, with feeling. Tell yourself:

> I give myself praise for my life as it is right now.
> I am always doing the best I can at any moment.
> I acknowledge myself for all the good I do.
> I recognize myself in this moment for being the wonderful person that I am.
> I use my words to praise myself, to praise the good in my life and to praise God.
> I find it easy to praise others for the good they do.

Thank you. Good work. See you tomorrow.

Day Seven
CHOOSING LOVE

Happy Self-Love Day! Welcome to Day 7 of the 21-Day Self-Love Mirror Work Experience. The energizing focusing of the day is CHOOSING LOVE.

In the recipe of love, you are the main ingredient. So many of us are under the impression that we are without love and it simply is not true. We can never be without love because we were created out of love and the Creator designed us out of a loving Presence. Our very existence is the expression of life's longing for itself, which is love. For this reason, it is impossible to ever be without love. However, if we believe that we are without it, then we live from the false belief that it is somewhere other than where we are.

It has been written, "Love is the beginning of all things." I agree and I believe that it begins within, so we must start with ourselves first. Love is a state of being, but we must consciously choose it if we are to enjoy its greatest benefits.

When love is present, things are different and when we choose love for ourselves from within, we become different. It's not about who doesn't love you that matters. It's about the love you have inside of you that you are willing to give yourself that matters most. Because, then and only then, can you love others from a healthy place, rather than seeking it outside of yourself, which can never sustain or fulfill you.

Starting today, make a conscious choice to be gentle, kind and patient with yourself. Treat yourself as lovingly as you would a dear friend.

Many times, we do not *choose* love. We, consciously or unconsciously, *choose* fear, anger, guilt, shame, criticism and judgment, but we must actively and proactively make the choice to experience love. Otherwise, it will be random in our experience.

In his book, *The Creator Speaks Book 1, The Book of Love*, Ken Banks encourages us to remember, "Your nature, your very being, the truest essence of you is woven in love, was created in love, exists in love." This is your inherent truth if you will simply believe.

The lyrics of one of Dionne Warwick's songs are "what the world needs now is love sweet love, it's the only thing there's just too little of." I believe the world is filled with people who do love. They love material goods. They love to receive praise from others. They love to receive acceptance from others. They love status. They love seeking the approval of others, but they are not willing to take the time to be with themselves, to love themselves wholly and fully. That's what there is too little of. When we have more individuals who are willing to practice self-love, then there will be more love expressed and felt on the planet.

Growth Work Exercise

Time to sit with yourself and your mirror. Looking into your beautiful eyes, breathing slowly, take seven deep-cleansing breaths before you begin. Affirm from your heart out loud:

> Today I choose love over fear.
> I choose to love me like never before.
> I choose to consider all the loving things that are true about me.
> I choose to remember the Creator created me out of Love.
> I choose to remember my very nature is love.
> I choose to remember my very being is love.

I choose to practice loving myself more and more every day because I realize, when I choose to love me, loving others is inevitable.

I am free to create a life of love.

Thank you. Good work. See you tomorrow.

WEEK TWO

Day Eight
LETTING GO

Happy Self-Love Day! Welcome to Day 8 of the 21-Day Self-Love Mirror Work Experience. The energizing focus of the day is LETTING GO!

Yesterday ended last night. If you are living in emotional pain, it is probably because you are living in the past. It's time to let go of your desire of the need for the past to be different than it was. Whatever happened then is not happening now. And more than likely, it was probably different than you remember it anyway. Feelings are not facts. Forgive yourself and everybody who you think did you wrong. At this moment, you are fine.

This personal inward journey is all about *you*. At least for the duration of this self-love experience, be willing to let go of any ill feelings you have towards yourself. Focus on what you have done that you need to forgive yourself for and let it go.

Holding on to unforgiveness is like holding a hot coal in the palm of your hand looking for somewhere to throw it. Let it go. Let it go *now*. It's burning your hand. It's tying up your energy. It's keeping you preoccupied in a way that is turning you away from joy and love.

By now, you are more than likely accustomed to the pain and it doesn't burn as much anymore. Nevertheless, you cannot use that hand to receive something more pleasurable. Drop it and allow your healing to begin. Enjoy the sweet release that comes from letting go. There is a healing balm that accompanies the act of forgiveness. Forgive yourself. Forgive others. Forgive everyone.

Growth Work Exercise

It's time for you to connect with yourself in the mirror. Gaze into your beautiful eyes. Just sit with yourself and notice what is coming up for you. What do you need to let go of today? Which story have you been telling yourself that is burning a hole in your dreams? Which stories are popping in your mind at this moment? Take a moment to jot each one down in your journal; not the long version of the story, just the title you have given it. Intuitively, you know the stories you remember that keep recurring in your life experiences. Yes, that one. As you think about the stories, allow your feelings to surface for each.

Take your time. It may be necessary to talk to your parents while looking in the mirror. Get it out. Have a dialogue with whomever you need to talk to in the mirror, even if the person is no longer living, even if they live in another state, even if they live in your home. Regardless, you and your best friend in the mirror are free to say what you need to say to help you let go.

This Self-Love Experience is all about you, so be patient with yourself. It is okay to cry if you need to. It is natural to do so during your mirror exercises. Grab a tissue and allow yourself to be with your feelings. Sit with them.

When you are ready, repeat these affirmations out loud, slowly and deliberately:

> Today I am letting go.
> I am fearless and brave.
> I have the courage to finally let go.
> I am letting go of all that no longer serves me.
> I am willing to let go of the patterns in my experiences that are getting in the way of me feeling unconditional love.

I am letting go of the stories that continue to wreak havoc on my life.

I am letting go of the false belief that I am unlovable because it is untrue.

I am letting go of judgments, criticisms, guilt, jealousy, shame, blame, anger and all my fears.

I am letting go of thoughts that suggest anything other than love.

I choose to focus on me and allow myself to be at peace.

It's okay and I'm okay.

I set myself free to create a life of unconditional love.

Thank you. Good work. See you tomorrow.

Day Nine
TRUST

Happy Self-Love Day! Welcome to the Day 9 of the 21-Day Self-Love Mirror Work Experience. The energizing focus of the day is TRUST.

One of my pearls of wisdom is "Love people; trust God." It can be easy to do the opposite of that and experience unnecessary betrayal by others. We have been encouraged to love our neighbors as ourselves, but it doesn't mean we have to trust them. Human beings are imperfect. Trusting them always to do what is in your best interest is unwise. Although people are doing the best they can, everybody's version of their best is subjective.

To trust means to have confidence, faith or hope in someone or something. We trust that the sun will rise in the morning. We trust it so much that we don't give much thought to the idea that it will not. In America, we trust that water and light will be there when we turn on the water faucet or the light switch. We trust that we'll take our next breath. We have confidence and faith in those outcomes. We even take it for granted.

Inscribed on our currency for this country are the words, "In God We Trust." I trust God and I trust the process of life. It has been my experience that God is faithful. And although I don't always understand what is happening or why, things always work out for me.

I have faith in God. I trust that I am one with the One. I trust the Universe. I trust there is a principle, a law backing all of life that corresponds and supports the evolution of all of humanity. I trust that life is unfolding in Divine right order. Yes, Divine right action is always taking place in spite of appearances.

When you choose to trust instead of fear, letting go and surrender are inevitable. Let go of control. Let go of the need to know. Let go of the need to be right. Let go of attachment to the outcome.

So, what does trusting the process look like? If your job ends, you know there is a much better one waiting. It means if an illness strikes, there is a newness and rebirth yearning to take place in you. It means if a relationship or someone's life ends, things don't actually die; they resurrect and give birth to something even more remarkable.

Trusting yourself is also key. Today is a perfect day to no longer commit emotional fraud with yourself. Your failures may be causing you not to trust yourself. However, those failures were the result of expecting something or someone beyond your consciousness to make your life work. Truth be told, when you place yourself, your heart, in the hands of others what happens to you is beyond your control. When you outsource what is best coming from within you, the outcome may or may not be in your favor. As you learn to love yourself first and honor yourself more, you will begin to trust yourself more and more. It takes time because you have a history of self-betrayal that may be in your consciousness. Before today, you put your trust in others.

In the present moment, you have made a decision to be the primary caregiver of your emotions. The time is now to take care of you and your emotions and allow others to do the same for themselves. It is important you no longer look to others as your source of happiness. Trust yourself.

Developing a sense of trust is vital. Without it, you will be riddled with anxiety, worry and fear, which block you from receiving your good.

Growth Work Exercise

Go into a relaxed state using deep breathing. And then say the affirmations below to yourself, really *feeling* them:

> I feel trust in my heart.
> I am willing to trust myself.
> I trust God and I trust the process.
> I trust good to flow into my life, through my life and that I am always in the flow.
> I trust that health, happiness and success are possible for me.
> I trust my own ability to take care of my emotions.
> I trust my expanding ability to create inner peace and joy in my life.
> I trust myself to create a life of unconditional love.
> I trust the Universal Mind to respond to my new beliefs.

Thank you. Good work. See you tomorrow.

Day Ten
RESPONSIBILITY

Happy Self-Love Day! Welcome to Day 10 of the 21-Day Self-Love Mirror Work Experience. The energizing focus of the day is SELF-RESPONSIBILITY.

When you blame others, you give away your power. Blaming others for your misery gets in the way of self-love. It is essential for you to take responsibility for the role you have played in your life.

Today, choose to own the choices you made. It was your decision or your indecision that produced what is in your life and be okay with that. Now that you know better, you can do better, so your life can be better. No one is to blame for your perceptions except you. No one is to blame for you handing over your life to someone else on a silver platter, hoping they would prioritize you over themselves. It seems to me that we expect way too much from others and way too little from ourselves.

Regardless of your relationship with another person, they are not responsible for your feelings. If they do not give you what you expect the way you expect it, it is your responsibility to give it to yourself. Most people are doing the best they can and, often, what we expect from others we are not willing to give to ourselves. Perhaps they are incapable of giving you what you expect or maybe they just don't want to. Forgive them and forgive yourself for expecting so much from them. Your parents, your partner, your children, your friends, your co-workers may be doing their best at the moment. In either case, they are not responsible for you or your feelings. You are. Practice self-responsibility by giving yourself what you need.

Today is a great day to heal your reliance on anything or anyone other than yourself and God. Tune in. You are the only one who gets to decide that. You can experience love in the way you want it. No one can do that for you better than you. So get to it. You are the best thing that ever happened to you. You are responsible for pleasing yourself, amusing yourself and renewing yourself.

Growth Work Exercise

Place your hand on your heart. Take some deep cleansing breaths. Sit in front of or pick up your mirror and say the following words with feeling:

> Today I accept full responsibility for my
> life and my well-being.
> I am responsible for myself.
> I find it easy to practice
> self-responsibility.
> Whenever I feel unloved, I go to my
> mirror and remind myself that I am
> loved, loving and lovable.
> I take responsibility for my thoughts
> and choose thoughts that support
> me. I take responsibility for my
> feelings and consciously choose to
> feel better whenever I don't.
> I take responsibility for my beliefs and
> choose new beliefs if the ones I
> have are no longer serving me.
> I take responsibility for my behavior and
> choose to demonstrate love with myself
> and others regardless of what is
> happening.

I take time to make a list of the many things that are loveable about me.

I take responsibility for myself and my experiences and choose to focus on God and not my problems.

I am responsible for creating my own wonderful life of unconditional love.

Thank you. Good work. See you tomorrow.

Day Eleven
WORTHINESS

Happy Self-Love Day! Welcome to Day 11 of the 21-Day Self-Love Mirror Work Experience. The energizing focus of the day is WORTHINESS.

Today, let's realize that we are worthy and we do not have to deserve good to experience our good.

Growing up, we may have learned that we had to earn love from our parents, teachers, friends and even God. At an early age, organized religion taught me that I was not one of the Chosen People; it described me as a Gentile. I also remember being taught that based on the original sin, I was undeserving. In addition to the church rhetoric, I grew up in the South, in Atlanta, Georgia, home and birthplace of the civil rights leader and activist, Dr. Martin Luther King, Jr. It was common to hear a teacher or a parent say that being Black meant I had to work twice as hard as my Caucasian friends in order to be accepted. All these outside influences were the ingredients of a nice recipe for the cake of inferiority for me early on. These untruths, stereotypes and fallacies were incongruent with the Truth of my being that I would later learn and practice. I didn't innately feel inadequate, but the outside world was suggesting these false ideas to me.

Today, we see commercials and advertisements that influence us to believe that we are not enough, that we are unworthy until and unless we attend a certain college, drive a certain car, live in a certain neighborhood, work at the right company, have a certain amount of money, net worth, or attain a certain status. In an effort to fit in or keep up with the Joneses and the Kardashians, to feel worthy, many people stress themselves out wearing labels to define themselves instead of knowing that being a child of the Most High is the most important label they need. This and this alone makes you and me enough. In fact, we are more than enough.

Things don't have worth in and of themselves. It is humanity who assigns value and worth to things, not the other way around. When we buy into the idea that outside things make us worthy or contribute to our worth, it not only creates discord within us; it fuels division between us. The same Higher Power that created everything created all of us. If that is not enough, I don't know what is.

You, me and everyone deserve God's goodness. We are all worthy. We were not created in the image and likeness of the Most High so that we can feel like we are not enough. Unworthiness is a byproduct of humanity's desire to create separation and division. There is only one race, the human race, and we were all created equal. We all have the same bodily organs. We bleed the same color blood. We all need breath to live and we all have the same access to God. The only difference is that some don't know their worth, while others do.

There is a universal principle that supports us as long as we believe we are supported. Each of us has the right to think, believe and feel that we deserve the best, that we are worthy. This is the way our hearts' desires make their appearance in our lives.

To experience the best, you must believe you deserve the best and no one can stop you from believing what you want to believe. The clergy may have said you don't deserve it, but what did God say? Many are double-minded when they pray. The idea of their unworthiness dilutes their faith in their desires.

Always believe you deserve the best and you will have exactly that. Everything comes to you from within your consciousness. Anything you feel and believe you don't deserve, that you are not worthy of, you automatically cut off from yourself.

Conversely, anything that you can actually and honestly think, feel and believe you are worthy of must come to you. In either case, you are right.

The material things we are socialized to give worth to are based solely on our common belief that it has worth. You have more *worth* than any "thing" that exists. Your worthiness is determined by your state of consciousness.

I invite you to change your idea of your worthiness. Your worth is not determined by anything outside of you. It is based purely on your consciousness about yourself and the God within. You do deserve the best and you are worthy of all good. Your heart beats and you breathe because you exist.

Growth Work Exercise

Tune in to the stillness within you by breathing slowly, deeply for one to two minutes. I invite you to open your heart and mind to the idea of your worthiness and affirm your truth by saying the following out loud in your mirror at least three (3) times.

> Today I accept that I am worthy of all good.
> I believe I am a good person who deserves
> good things.

My self-worthiness is a result of how I see myself.

My self-worth and value comes from within me.

What I think about myself is what determines how worthy I feel.

What I feel about myself is what determines how worthy I feel.

What I believe about myself is what determines how worthy I feel.

My worthiness depends on what I think about myself within myself.

My worthiness depends on how I feel about myself within myself.

My worthiness depends on what I believe about myself within myself.

What other people think about me is none of my business.

What other people say about me is none of my business.

What other people believe about me is none of my business.

I release the need to feel bound by what other people think, say or believe about me.

The idea of my unworthiness is a false self-identity that no longer serves me.

Therefore, I treat myself with value.

I accept that I am important.
I accept that I am enough.
I accept that I am valuable and worthy.
I talk to myself in a kind and caring manner.
I am patient with myself.
I take great care of myself in all ways.
I celebrate my good qualities.
I shower myself with acceptance and love.
This is my truth today and always.
And so it is.

Thank you. Good work. See you tomorrow.

Day Twelve
HONESTY

Happy Self-Love Day! Welcome to Day 12 of the 21-Day Self-Love Mirror Work Experience. The energizing focus of the day is HONESTY.

It is said that honesty is the best policy, but let's tweak it a bit. Self-honesty is best. Be honest about what you believe in. Be honest about what hurts you. Be honest about what you feel. Be open and honest when communicating with yourself and others. If someone invites you to be a part of something, check-in with yourself to determine if it is okay with your inner self. If not, say no to them and yes to yourself.

Self-honesty is paramount. When you are honest with yourself and others, you are in a place of integrity with yourself. The moment you are out of integrity with yourself, you compromise your integrity with others. You owe it to yourself to keep your word with yourself, to be honest with yourself at all times.

Otherwise, you engage in self-betrayal and self-love is no longer happening for you. Have the courage to always be honest with yourself and it will be easier for you to be honest with others. When you are honest with yourself, you attract honest relationships and experiences in your life.

In my life experiences, I found it easy to keep my word with others and learned that sometimes I did so at the expense of being in integrity with myself. It can be easy to be a person of integrity who does not practice self-integrity. When this happens, you create dissonance within and, before you know it, you will be at odds with yourself. Self-integrity is a prerequisite to your self-love practice.

Some things that motivate us to be dishonest with ourselves in our relationships with others include the fear of no longer having that person in our lives or the fear of disappointing them or making them angry. Or because we love them, we feel responsible for them or we don't want to feel guilty. Believe it or not, these are all reasons we may betray honesty with ourselves in an effort to preserve our relationships with others although the relationships may be unhealthy, especially if they are family members.

We must be honest and true to ourselves before

we can be honest and true to anyone else. In all things, honor yourself first and leave room for others to do the same. Honor yourself and practice self-honesty at all times.

Growth Work Exercise

Have a seat with your mirror. Breathe in, breathe out. Slowly breathe in through your nose and out through your mouth for two to three minutes. Looking into your mirror, with your hands on your heart, say the following words aloud:

> My beautiful soul is crying out to be honored, and I give it the attention it needs.
> I am open to being my own best friend and honesty is the cornerstone of my friendship with myself.
> I know that self-honesty is the best policy for me.
> It is easy for me to be honest with myself.
> It is easy for me to be honest with others.
> I practice honesty every day.
> I am healing myself.
> Now that I am ready for change and willing to do the work, I honor myself first and inner peace follows.

I am now building a healthy and loving relationship with the most important person I will ever meet—Me.

By being honest with myself, I am creating a life of unconditional love.

Being honest with myself makes me happy.

I am so grateful.

Thank you. Good work. See you tomorrow.

Day Thirteen
BEAUTY

Happy Self-Love Day! Welcome to Day 13 of the 21-Day Self-Love Mirror Work Experience. The energizing focus of the day is BEAUTY.

You are beautiful, so full of beauty. Walk the path of beauty. Relish and encourage its inward and outward expressions. Acknowledge the radiance of the creation who is you.

Isaiah 61:1-3 describes the exchange of a crown of beauty for ashes, oil of joy for mourning and a garment of praise for despair. This passage communicates that we can clothe ourselves in splendor, but we must be open to change and exchange. We are encouraged to choose. You can't keep the beauty *and* the ashes; you get to have one or the other. We must choose and our lives will respond in accordance with whichever we accept. We do have a choice.

Let's radiate beauty. There are personal and

professional experiences that alter us for life. These are the ashes mentioned in the scripture. Ashes are an altered state of something that has been burned. And so many have been burned by their painful life experiences. Abuse and abandonment have impacted so many. It's probably fair to say we have all been impacted by some form of abuse, whether directly or indirectly. It may not have happened to you, but it may have happened to someone you know. Some types of abuse you may have witnessed or experienced firsthand may include verbal, emotional, physical, or mental abuse. I can recall my own experience with corporate bullying in the workplace. Working in a hostile environment impacted my emotional state of being. Some homes, schools, churches and workplaces foster a hostile environment.

As a result of the many variations of abuse, many people are brokenhearted and their souls are wounded. Many have experienced deep hurt, abandonment, rejection, betrayal, self-pity, bitterness, criticism, judgment, shame and guilt. The evidence of misery and suffering is rampant and can be linked to a world full of people who have addictions of all kinds—drug, alcohol, shopping, food, work, and the list goes on and on—to escape the pain.

Mass media—movies, television, radio, and all

social platforms—has exposed us to so much. Consequently, we bear witness to society's ills and can lose sight of humanity's beauty. Be clear beauty is all around us, but we must give our attention to it to see and experience it.

Don't allow someone else's ugliness to tarnish your beauty. No matter what has been done or said to you, you are full and filled with beauty. You no longer have to sit in the prison of your mind because the door is unlocked. All you have to do is make a decision to stand up and walk away from anything that does not reflect your inner beauty. When are you going to forgive those who hurt you? I know you think it's hard and that it's not fair, but *now* is the perfect time to begin to allow the beauty within you to shine. Don't let what happened to you become an excuse to stay the way you are. Feeling hurt and living from that space is hurting you. It's okay to admit that you are not okay, but it's not okay to be okay with not being okay.

During this Mirror Work Experience, we are walking it out together. You are getting the opportunity to speak to the God in you every single day. The secret place of the Most High is within you. Go to that place and tap into the indwelling Presence within and allow it to heal your wounded soul. You are beautiful and nothing that you have experienced can ever change that truth. But you must see it for yourself. It is necessary for you to cosign and agree that you are. You are created in the spiritual image and likeness of the Creator. How could you be anything other than beautiful?

So, let's walk it out! It's time to set yourself free. See your way out by seeing your way through. The mirror in front of you is here to help you see the beauty you are inside, regardless of what may have happened to you.

The most important day in your life is *today*!

Growth Work Exercise

It's time to go within. Breathe deep. Breathe slowly. Breathe gently. As you inhale and exhale to center yourself, bring yourself to the present moment. Give yourself at least three to five minutes to connect within. When you are ready, please repeat the following:

> Today I am open to divine exchange.
> I accept beauty in exchange for ashes.
> I accept joy in exchange for mourning.
> I accept praise in exchange
> for depression. I accept
> respect in exchange for shame.

I accept forgiveness in
exchange for blame.
I accept hope in exchange for despair.
I accept innocence for guilt.
I gladly exchange beauty for ashes.
I allow my ashes to be scattered
and to dissolve.
I choose to renew my mind, emotions,
heart and spirit.
I am creating a wonderful life of beauty
and unconditional love.
I deserve it.

Thank you. Good work. See you tomorrow.

Day Fourteen
COMMITMENT

Happy Self-Love Day!!! Welcome to Day 14 of the 21-Day Self-Love Mirror Work Experience. The energizing focus of the day is COMMITMENT.

Keeping your commitments with yourself is an act of self-love. It can be easy to commit to others because of the short-term benefits of their approval. We have been taught from early childhood to seek praise and approval from parents, teachers, clergy, lovers, friends, etc.

We have been domesticated to honor the commitments we make with others *above* the commitments we make with ourselves. And sometimes, the two are in conflict with each other. Our family, the church, the workplace, etc., send us the message to put the needs of others before our own. When you honor your commitment with yourself first, you can more easily and joyfully honor your commitments with others. It all begins with you. When you prioritize yourself, you will feel alignment from within and resentment at a later time will be a nonissue.

Hindsight is 20/20. During my eighteen-year relationship with my ex-husband, I learned a great lesson about commitment. I was committed to the marriage, my husband and my twin daughters first over and *above* my commitment to myself. Little did I know that leaving myself out of the equation was unhealthy and was not sustainable.

Soon after my divorce, I was gifted a wonderful book that would forever change my life. *The Gift of Taking* by Dr. Jill Kahn masterfully makes the need for commitment to yourself very clear. She says, "Honor yourself and all else will follow. So many of us were taught from an early age to think of others first. But the answers are all mirrored in nature. Even though a tree gives us oxygen, shade, wood and fruit, it must "take" what it needs first—energy from the sun, nutrients from the soil and water to replenish itself. Then to maintain balance, it overflows its surplus as the gift of oxygen—our breath for life."

Honoring ourselves and our commitments to ourselves is nature's lesson for us to follow. Dr. Kahn's book and her coaching helped me to understand and practice keeping commitments with myself. I learned to honor myself first and allow others to do the same for themselves. The application of this universal principle helped me to have healthier relationships personally and professionally.

The long-term benefits of maintaining personal commitments with ourselves are so rewarding. There is unbridled inner peace and joy that surpasses all understanding. You are now learning to cultivate a loving, committed relationship with the most important person you will ever meet—yourself.

Growth Work Exercise

Have a seat or stand in front of your mirror. Take a look into the eyes of the best friend you will ever have. Let's make a personal commitment here and now. Repeat these words slowly, out loud and with sincere feelings:

> Today I make a personal commitment with myself.
> I take you (insert your name) as my friend and love, in laughter and in tears, in conflict and tranquility, asking that you be no one other than yourself.
> I promise to love you and cherish you for as long as we both shall live.

I value my commitment to you and take it very seriously.

I make the commitment to be responsible for my own happiness.

I make the commitment to learn how to love myself more.

I make the commitment to learn how to appreciate myself more.

I make the commitment to learn how to be good to myself.

I make the commitment to let go of anything and anybody who is unhealthy for me.

I make the commitment to see obstacles as opportunities and to grow and expand.

I make the commitment to no longer allow the feelings and attitudes of others to affect my success or my future.

I make the commitment to be patient with myself.

I make the commitment to schedule myself on my calendar for self-care and time to have fun.

I love and honor my beautiful relationship with me.

Thank you. Good work. See you tomorrow.

WEEK THREE

Day Fifteen
LOVING YOUR INNER CHILD

Happy Self-Love Day! Welcome to Day 15 of the 21-Day Self-Love Mirror Work Experience. The energizing focus of the day is LOVING YOUR INNER CHILD.

Today, let's take care of our inner child. As children, what we wanted more than anything was to be loved and accepted as we were. That's still what all of us want only we're not going to get it until we are willing to give it to ourselves first. The changes we want are going to have to come through us not from outside of us.

The inner child is the part of us that carries all the negative messages from the past and, although there may be happy messages in there too, the negative ones are what limit us today. For this reason, it is very helpful to get in touch with the part of us that feels unloved and not good enough.

Early childhood memories are often etched in your heart like initials engraved on a locket that will endure the test of time. They live in us, never to be forgotten. They become the leading reason why we do what we do the way we do it.

Have you ever wondered why you are the way you are? Or why you are attracted to certain people and not others? Or why you have certain preferences? Engaging with your inner child can help you to understand why.

As adults, many of us spend a lifetime trying to avoid the pain we experienced during childhood. If we are to embrace the hope of a better life, we must move beyond childhood experiences that may include pain and trauma. The mental baggage we carry from childhood can be heavy and has a hefty price.

We all have an inner child who has been hurt and wounded in some way by others. The experiences can lead you to believe you are a victim. They can lead you to blame others. They can disempower you.

In search of healing and wholeness, we must be willing to love our younger self unconditionally no matter what happened to him or her. You cannot heal what you cannot feel. Repeat these words, "I need to feel in order to heal!"

We cannot be whole if we are rejecting any parts of ourselves. The integration of your younger self with your adult self will help you to become whole. If you are unwilling to move past hurtful childhood memories, you cannot enjoy the benefits of inner harmony and inner peace.

We have all picked up ideas along the journey of childhood. Many times the things others said to us as children taught us to believe that we were not okay or that we were inadequate in some way. We may have received false messages from a parent, teacher, relative, another child or clergyman. No matter who it was, we may have unknowingly given others the authority to influence our own opinions of ourselves. We falsely believed their words were more powerful than our own.

As children, we may have told ourselves stories to survive. We watched, we heard, we felt. Children don't usually tell anyone what they are thinking, but the stories we tell ourselves shape our lives. We base everything in our lives on the feedback we received from our childhood experiences and interactions. This is why it is in our best interest to be open to healing our inner child today.

What happened to us as children is contained inside of us. Therefore, inner-child work is paramount. Childhood may have influenced us to believe there's something missing or there's something wrong. Today I say to you, there is nothing missing and there is nothing wrong. As children we may have felt disempowered and that there was nothing we could do about it. But today is a new day. Mirror Work works wonders. It works if you work it.

How others saw me and treated me used to shape my own opinion of myself, but not anymore. Today, you don't have to live based on what other people do to and say about you. If how you feel depends on others, you'll continue to live a life of anxiety and fear. You will be anxious and afraid.

If you are ready to completely be who you are, you must begin to love your hurting inner child who deserves your unconditional love. So, let's have an intimate conversation with yourself today in the mirror with your best friend.

Please understand that inner-child work can be very emotional, so be patient with yourself. And, if you can't remember anything from your childhood, just relax during this exercise and say to yourself, "Anything I need to know comes to me."

Let's use the mirror to connect with our inner selves. This powerful connection reveals the beliefs within us that need to be cleared. Remember, when you notice your feelings in the mirror, be sure not to judge or criticize them. Just notice what you are feeling. Let's be willing to give ourselves the unconditional love and attention we deserve. Let's be willing to love ourselves just the way we are, right here and now. Give yourself a hug and let's get started.

Growth Work Exercise

Take a moment and find the youngest photo of yourself, preferably one where your eyes are open. Grab your journal, a pen, tissues and sit in front of your mirror.

Holding your childhood photo, gaze into the eyes of this beautiful child you are looking at. If you don't have a photo, close your eyes and picture yourself as a child. Breathe slowly, gently, deeply. Inhale and exhale, allowing yourself to connect with your younger self. Continue breathing. Take your time.

How are you feeling about the child you are connecting with? What are that child's eyes saying to you at this moment? Listen with love. Your heart knows what that child felt and what the child within you is still feeling today. Yes, I know someone may have hurt you and you are holding on to the hurt you felt. But it is time to release the pain and leave the experience where it happened — in the past. Your inner child no longer wants to be protected by you;

he or she is ready to be loved and acknowledged by you instead. Your inner child no longer wants to feel scared and alone. Unfortunately, no one you know or meet today will be able to fill the void or heal that child within you except you.

Here are your affirmations for the day. Say them out loud in the mirror. Feel the words as you say them:

> I now have the courage and compassion to embrace and love you, little (your name).
> I understand and am aware that you are part of me.
> Today I am creating a safe space for you in my life little (your name).
> I am happy to get to know you better.
> I want you to learn to trust me.
> I am willing to love you with all my heart from now on.
> I promise to show you more love.

Take several deep breaths as you continue to tell your inner child the following:

> I love you little (your name).
> I care about you.

I love you more than you may
ever know.
You mean the world to me.
I am here for you from now on.
How can I help you feel happy today?

No one can love you more than you. This is why self-love is so important. At a later time, perhaps on the weekend, write a love letter to your inner child. Begin with "Dear Beloved Inner Child, Little (insert your name)! You are the love of my life."

Thank you. Good work. See you tomorrow.

Day Sixteen
RELEASING ANGER

Happy Self-Love Day! Welcome to Day 16 of the 21-Day Self-Love Mirror Work Experience. The energizing focus of the day is RELEASING ANGER.

Anger takes up space in the body where positive emotions want to live.

Many of us didn't have very good role models to teach us how to express and release anger in a healthy way. But our bodies literally store these emotions until they are expressed. During our Self-Love Mirror Work Experience, we are open to healing. It is the perfect time to become aware of our stored feelings so that we can express and release them.

How was anger handled when you were growing up? How do you handle it now? Have you ever noticed that you tend to get most angry with the people you love and care about the most? This is normal. Those closest to us really know how to push our buttons.

To amend means to heal. It's time to unlock the chains around your heart. Who offended you? Who angered you? Are you allowing those offenses from early childhood to hurt you today or dictate your life? Or perhaps you are angry with someone who hurt you in adulthood. You may even be angry with yourself. In either case, anger that is suppressed is harmful to you emotionally, mentally, spiritually and physically. It consumes your mind, alters your spirit and can create dis-ease in your body.

There is no need to feel bad about being angry. However, what's important is learning how to effectively channel it out of your body. Physical exercise can help you relieve your body of stored emotions. Hitting and yelling into a pillow is definitely a great way to relieve the tension as well. It also helps to talk about what makes you angry. Therapy, Coaching and Mirror Work are excellent ways to talk through your anger if you are not able to talk to the person you are angry with. Just be sure you take a positive approach to channel your anger. It is never okay to strike another person or to self-harm when you feel angry.

Growth Work Exercise

So, let's take care of yourself. Remember you have a choice today. Close your eyes. Inhale through your mouth, hold it, now push it out of your mouth with force. Again, breathe in through your mouth to the count of four and hold it for a count of four. Now blow it out strongly. Do this at least five times. I recommend three to five minutes while looking into your eyes in the mirror. We are releasing anger. And it's okay to cry. Repeat the following at least ten times:

> It's okay for me to feel, express and release my feelings.
> It's okay for me to feel, express and release my feelings.
> It's okay for me to feel, express and release my feelings.
> I am willing to release the anger I have been holding in my heart from the past.
> I am willing to release the anger I have in my heart towards others.
> I am willing to release the anger I have in my heart toward myself.

So, "who's" the matter with you? Usually, our

anger is associated with a person and whenever we see or think of them, the anger shows up. For this next exercise, fill in the blanks below by saying out loud in your mirror the name of the person and why you are angry. You may be one of the people you are angry with. If so, place your name in the blank where necessary. Take your time and complete the following sentences until you can think of no one else and nothing else. Here are six listed here to get you started.

_____ I am angry at you because
_____.

_____ I am angry at you because
_____.

_____ I am angry at you because
_____.

_____ I am angry at you because
_____.

_____ I am angry at you because
_____.

_____ I am angry at you because
_____.

Close your eyes as you take more, deep cleansing breaths. Breathe in and exhale slowly to allow the anger to be released and dissipate. Healing takes time. Please take as much time as you need.

Now when you are ready, please say the following out loud to your best friend in the mirror:

> I release bitterness and fear.
> I release anger and anxiety.
> I no longer blame others.
> I relax and let go of it all.
> My peace of mind is restored.
> There is peace in my heart.
> I set myself free.
> I am creating a wonderful life of unconditional love.
> Thank you, God.

Give yourself a big hug in the mirror.

Thank you. Good work. See you tomorrow.

Day Seventeen
COMPASSION

Happy Self-Love Day! Welcome to Day 17 of the 21-Day Self-Love Mirror Work Experience. The energizing focus of the day is SELF-COMPASSION.

The Buddhist understanding of compassion means offering patience, kindness, and non-judgmental understanding to others as well as *oneself.* Notice one's self is included. Contrary to what you might have been taught to believe, self-compassion is not equivalent to selfishness.

> *"You can search throughout the entire universe for someone who is more deserving of your love and affection than you are yourself, and that person is not to be found anywhere. You yourself, as much as anybody*

in the entire universe deserve your love and affection."

—Buddha

An easy way to understand self-compassion is to consider the instructions given by flight attendants to put your oxygen mask on *before* helping someone else with theirs. We need to make sure we take care of ourselves before offering care to others.

Self-compassion is best practiced with self-awareness and understanding. We must make sure we are aware of our own needs, with the understanding that our own needs are a priority. Furthermore, we must be aware that we don't have to do anything special to deserve love; and understand that we do not need to be a certain way to be worthy of love, nor do we need to earn it.

Two key benefits of self-compassion are that it minimizes self-judgment and will help you turn your inner critic into a gentle supporter. When confronted with shortcomings, you will no longer punish yourself. Instead, you will see obstacles as opportunities for growth and inner healing. You will be more encouraging to yourself self. You will begin to feel safe with yourself as you begin to treat yourself as a dear friend.

As you cultivate a more loving connection with

yourself, you will have less negative self-talk and have more kind, supportive thoughts that help you to behave more lovingly toward yourself. Believe it or not, self-compassion is positively correlated with improved mental health and greater life satisfaction.

Our mirror work journey is helping us change the ways in which we view and treat ourselves, particularly in relation to others. One fine quality of compassion is generosity to others. However, for generosity to work in favor of your well-being, it cannot be selfless. So, when being generous, make sure you are aware of your own needs first, then consciously choose the recipient of your generosity and the resources you have available. Have fun being generous and be mindful that doing good for others makes us happy, but only if it does not reduce our levels of well-being. Be sure not to ignore your own needs. Self-compassion is all about how we relate to ourselves and how we relate to others.

It can be easy to express compassion for others and leave yourself out. However, self-compassion is mandatory to practice unconditional self-love. Self-compassion empowers you to take skillful action to show love to yourself by being kind, loving, patient and accepting with yourself just as you are. When you cultivate compassion for yourself, you add peace to your life and increase your happiness quotient. When you are happy, it helps you to be a cheerful giver to others, but you must not leave yourself out.

People who have self-compassion also have *greater social connectedness, emotional intelligence, happiness,* and overall life satisfaction. Self-compassion is also known to correlate with less anxiety, depression, shame, and fear of failure.

Growth Work Exercise

Center yourself with your breath work. Take five slow, deep cleansing breaths or take three to five minutes to quiet your mind. Using your mirror, I invite you to place your hand on your heart and read the following out loud in your mirror:

> I enjoy giving to others.
> Doing good for others makes me happy.
> It is fun to be generous and I always remember to start with myself.
> I demonstrate a loving spirit to everyone I meet.
> I treat everyone fairly.
> I have a positive attitude at all times.
> I offer help to others when I feel guided to do so without being asked.

I am open and receptive to compassion being shown to me.

I understand that it is healthy for me to be good to myself and doing so helps me to be good to others.

I include myself when expressing compassion to others.

I am learning to be kind to myself.

I find it easy to practice self-compassion.

I now allow self-compassion to help me to create a wonderful life of unconditional love.

I am thankful.

Thank you. Good work. See you tomorrow.

Day Eighteen
REVERENCE

Happy Self-Love Day! Welcome to Day 18 of the 21-Day Self-Love Mirror Work Experience. The energizing focus of the day is REVERENCE.

Ronald Gross in *Socrates' Way: Seven Keys to Using Your Mind to the Utmost* wrote, "Practice reverence for life. The Sacred is in, with and under all the things of the world. Respond with appropriate respect and awe." Show respect for the environment, animals, the ocean and all things and when you see a spider, a bug, or bumblebee practice reverence. Show respect and regard for it and notice what happens. The same reverence you give is the same reverence you will experience. Reverence will be reflected back to you. When respect is given, then it can be received. This is the universal law of life. You reap what you sow.

Recently, I was with a friend when a bumblebee

began to buzz around us. She immediately began to swing at it and to resist its presence. Her resistance to the bee was drawing it to her. What you resist, persists.

I have always loved and revered nature. There is a wasp nest on my back deck. They build a new one every year. I have communicated verbally and in spirit that I will respect their humble abode as long as they respect mine. I have no problems with the wasps or the spiders that take, up residence on my deck. As a result, spiders, bugs, and bees don't bother or harm me. I show reverence for their life and they reflect reverence back to me. If one of them enters my home, I open the door or window and invite it to leave and it always does so with no hassle. This is reverence for life.

Years ago, I participated in a Sit Spot with a Shaman for thirty days. It is by far one of the most impactful things I have ever done. It attuned my mind, spirit, emotions and body for peace and consciously transformed my connection with nature.

I learned to cultivate present-moment awareness. Here's how it worked. I went to the same spot in nature every day. I sat on the ground in the grass for a minimum of twenty minutes and consciously observed nature—the trees, birds, squirrels, etc. There is a distinct difference between *seeing* a bird and *watching* a bird. It enhanced my sensitivity to nature and increased my reverence for it. I noticed toward the end of my sit-spot program how nature's inhabitants would approach me because this dynamic form of meditation reduced my human footprint in a way that made the birds, chipmunks and squirrels feel safe to be near me. My reverence and respect for life was reflected back to me in high definition. It felt like an awakening because I became much more aware of myself, my surroundings, and my next moves for my life and my business. I began to engage and experience life at a higher level physically, emotionally and spiritually.

Growth Work Exercise

With your mirror, relax, breathe and tune in. Reverence this moment by giving attention to your natural pattern of breathing. Just notice what you feel inside both physically and emotionally as you gaze into your eyes. Reverence the connection you feel with yourself. Say:

> As a being of light, I now practice reverence and kindness for all.
> I have great reverence for the Creator.
> I have great reverence for all that the Creator has created.

I show respect for myself.

I show respect for others.

And in return I receive respect.

I value life. I value my life. I value the lives of others.

I am an advocate of love and respect for all living things.

Because I revere my life, I treat myself kindly and lovingly always.

I cherish myself, my ideas, my desires, my body and my mind.

I listen intently and follow through with the passions of my own heart.

I no longer dismiss myself in any way.

I show honor to myself and others for I know that I am one with Life.

Thank you. Good work. See you tomorrow.

Day Nineteen
TAKE CARE OF YOUR BODY

Happy Self-Love Day! Welcome to Day 19 of the 21-Day Self-Love Mirror Work Experience. The energizing focus of the day is TAKE CARE OF YOUR BODY!

Your body houses your spirit. Growing up, I was taught that my body was the temple where God resides. Therefore, it has always been my intention and deep desire to keep my spirit pure. For this reason, I have made a conscious effort to be good to my body.

Your state of mind is important in relation to your body. I have always been mindful of the importance of daily exercise, healthy eating and what I allow to influence my mind. For at least twenty minutes a day, I do some form of exercise and am conscious of it as I am doing it. I am fully present.

My desire to cherish and revere the temple I live in has influenced me to be a conscious eater. As a conscious eater, I am mindful of what I eat, when I eat, how much I eat and my emotions when I am eating. Make healthy food choices by listening to your body's messages based on what feed your body. There is a mind-body connection that contributes to our wellness and wellbeing. Pay attention to what your body is telling you.

Many believe if they are vegan or vegetarian, they will have optimal health. However, if you eat healthy foods but have toxic thoughts or your state of mind is sad, anxious or troubled, you are not accessing maximum health. It's equally important to pay attention to what you feed your mind. Believe it or not, there are those who don't eat healthy or take great care of their bodies, but they take great care of their minds and spirit and live long happy lives.

Optimal health includes body, mind and spirit. It is imperative that we take care of our bodies and treat them as the precious creations they are. Your body's health is important because it houses your spirit. So, maintain a healthy state of being by being good to your body. Sleep, rest, relax and exercise daily. Find out the right exercise for your body type. Educate yourself about nutrition. Learn about foods so you can make the best decisions for yourself. Notice the kind of fuel you put into your body and the results you get. Eat foods that energize you. A great question to ask is yourself is, *what does my body need in order to experience optimal health and vitality?*

Growth Work Exercise

Center yourself with your breath. After five deep, cleansing breaths in and out, give attention to your body as you gaze into your eyes. Notice how you feel in this moment. Ask your body what message it wants to communicate to you. What emotion is being held in your body? And where is it being held? If there is any discomfort in your body, release it now. Breathe. Give thanks.

Now let's affirm the following:

> I love myself, so I take great
> care of my body.
> In this moment, I accept my body just the
> way it is and I am open to it getting
> better.

I exercise daily.
My body is getting stronger and
stronger everyday.
I recognize my body as a good friend.
Every cell in my body has
divine intelligence.
I listen to what it tells me and know
that its advice is valid.
It is easy for me to make healthy
food choices that nourish my mind,
body and spirit.
I love my body so I feed it good foods.
I notice the foods that energize me.
The divine intelligence within me guides
me to eat the proper diet.
I no longer condemn the foods I eat.
The foods I eat agree with me and I agree
with them.
Everything that I eat is perfectly assimi-
lated and perfectly eliminated.
There is perfect harmony with all that I
take into my physical body.
I now choose to be more accepting of my
body.
I love my body and my body loves me.
Every cell in my body is alive with health
and energy.

I move and exercise my body in ways that feel good.
My immune system is strong.
My body has a remarkable capacity for healing.
I love and respect my body always.

Thank you. Good work. See you tomorrow.

Day Twenty
RECEPTIVITY

Happy Self-Love Day. Welcome to Day 20 of the 21-Day Self-Love Mirror Work Experience. The energizing focus of the day is RECEPTIVITY.

Many people like to give love but may not be as good at receiving love from others. Now that you are learning to love yourself unconditionally, you will notice love being reflected back to you. Sometimes love from others comes in the form of a compliment. Have you ever been given a compliment and you deflected it by saying, "This old thing?" Or by downplaying it in some way? Other times you may be offered a gift. Has someone ever offered to pay for your meal and you refused the gift? Now that you are practicing unconditional self-love, the next time someone compliments you or invites you to a free meal, simply say, "Thank you."

When you are not receptive to the gifts extended

to you, you are communicating that you don't deserve what is being offered or you are saying you are unworthy of it. Neither is true. If you offered someone a gift from the kindness of your heart, not only would it make them happy, it would make you feel happy too. However, if they did not receive it, it would not feel good to you. The same is true for someone who may be offering you the gift of a compliment or something they thought you might enjoy. Be receptive to your good.

Consider as you do today's Mirror Work Exercise that you must receive oxygen when you inhale to live. You naturally receive sunlight when you go outside. And when someone smiles at you or says hello, you are receiving their kindness. Become aware of the many gifts available to you. Become receptive to them and notice how good it feels to receive. This is one of the many ways to practice self-love. When you are receptive to the good being offered to you, you open yourself to love.

Growth Work Exercise

Take a moment to be still. You may want to close your eyes. Give your undivided attention to your breathing. Slowly, inhale and exhale for at least five minutes. Now open your eyes and look within. Notice how you are feeling in this moment. Notice how you are receptive to the oxygen that is provided for you to breathe. Today is the 20th day of the 21 Day Self-Love Mirror Work Experience. You are almost finished. You have received many treasures during our journey together. As you continue breathing slowly and deeply, reflect on some of the gifts you received. What have you learned about yourself during your inner journey you did not know before? Are you happy you took the journey within?

Please say the following affirmations using your mirror:

> I am receptive to my good.
> I receive my good now.
> Good things happen to me every day.
> I deserve to have good in every
> area of my life.
> I open my heart to receive the goodness
> in store for me.
> I open my mind to receive the goodness
> in store for me.
> I now receive the unconditional love that
> is available to me today and I see this

love in every direction that I look.
I am thankful.

Thank you. Good work. See you tomorrow.

Day Twenty-One
LOVE YOURSELF, NOW AND ALWAYS!

Happy Self-Love Day! Welcome to Day 21 of the 21-Day Self-Love Mirror Work Experience. The energizing focus of the day is LOVE YOURSELF NOW AND ALWAYS.

CONGRATULATIONS! You deserve a big round of applause. You did it! You stuck with it and completed the 21-Day Self-Love Mirror Work Experience. You honored your commitment to yourself and opened yourself to learn how to accept, approve, appreciate and love yourself more. By now, you have compassion for yourself like never before. You have been establishing, developing and cultivating a deeper relationship with the most important person in your life—YOU. This new relationship with your best friend will always be with you so I encourage you to continue to share quality time with yourself daily.

You are the one you have been waiting for. For the last three weeks, you have taken a voyage within. There is a human tendency to seek love outside of ourselves when the truth is we can always look within. You and the Father are one. The mirror technique gave you the opportunity to communicate with the indwelling Presence within you. If you are looking for love, no need to look any further than the person you see looking back at you in the mirror.

On this journey, I hope you have learned to be loving to your negatives. I hope you realize and acknowledge they were not obstacles rather opportunities to grow and expand yourself. Now that you have demonstrated your willingness to love yourself, I believe you have found new, positive ways to enjoy your life with yourself.

When you pour love into you, your life will reflect that love back to you in the same way the mirror reflects back to you the image it sees in front of it. Life will give you love in return, but it can only return to you what you give to it. This is the law of reciprocity. It reciprocates what it is given. You reap what you sow and it all begins with you.

I encourage you to fall in love over and over and over again every day with You. Love yourself deeply, fully and completely, and notice how easily that love is reflected back to you. Notice how naturally you share love with others. And don't stop with humans. Love nature, the environment, plants, animals and the process of life and living. See LOVE everywhere you look.

You are a human being and love is a state of being-ness. You don't have to do anything to have love except to remember and acknowledge you have it because you are it. Technically, you can never be without it.

Growth Work Exercise

Today, sit in front of your mirror and notice how you feel. Do you feel a sense of accomplishment? You kept your word with yourself. How does that make you feel? Are you feeling better on Day 21 than you did on Day 1 of this Self-Love Experience? I hope so.

Take a deep cleansing breath and repeat the following affirmations:

> It's an extraordinary day.
> I open my heart to myself.
> I love and accept myself
> exactly the way I am.
> I deserve all good.

I am worthy of a wonderful life.

I easily release the past and move forward with joy.

I love myself more deeply every day.

I am willing to be kind and gentle with myself.

Loving myself makes it easier for me to love others.

When I share love, it comes back to me multiplied abundantly.

I am willing to accept love.

I experience acceptance everywhere I go.

I enjoy wonderful associations with positive, uplifting people.

I express my feelings openly and easily.

The love I extend returns to me multiplied.

Loving myself is a way of life!

I encourage you to continue to use the mirror to build your relationship with your forever friend. I highly recommend doing this self-love experience at least once a year. And definitely share it with someone you think is ready to take the journey within to discover who they are and how lovable they are.

You've only just begun.

Conclusion

For the last three weeks for a total of twenty-one days, you developed a spiritual practice of conscious contact with your inner self. You were able to pour into yourself and take care of yourself. I imagine that you feel a little more self-love than when you began. It is my hope that you:

- Have faced and overcome dilemmas in your relationship with yourself from childhood
- Unhooked and released hurt, pain, anguish, anger and resentment
- No longer feel incomplete and disconnected
- Can accept what you became aware of
- Are now building a better self-image
- Have experienced an awakening
- Are reawakening to your spiritual magnificence
- Feel fearless and free

The first law of nature is self-preservation. Nature teaches us that we must preserve ourselves in order to be beneficial to anyone or anything else. If you want to be able to share love and build healthy relationships with others, then you must preserve yourself by pouring love into yourself *first*. The abundance of love within you is more easily shared with others when you begin within. And, when you do, you will enjoy the love that is returned to you multiplied abundantly.

You gave yourself the great opportunity to heal and love yourself like never before. This 21-Day Self-Love Mirror Work Experience was an opportunity to open your consciousness to create a life of unconditional love so you can create a life that you love. By no longer looking for love outside of yourself to make you better, you now know you can never be without love because it is the totality of who you are. This process united you with the most important person you will ever meet and love, YOU. I trust you were able to let go of the false image you may have had and see yourself with eyes of love.

One great benefit of the 21-Day Self-Love Mirror Work Experience was to reach a harmonious state of spiritual awareness. Hopefully, your stream of consciousness opened you to the awareness about all there is to love about you.

One Moment of Genuine Self-Love

"I have an everyday religion that works for me. Love yourself first, and everything else falls into line."

—Lucille Ball

Loving yourself is your biggest gift to others. Everything you think and feel about others will change when you learn to embrace and love yourself. On the surface, it may sound like loving yourself is a selfish act, but it is actually self-responsibility. When you love the unlovable parts of yourself—anger, fear, grief, jealousy or whatever else—the problem you have with the other person clears up. If you take a few minutes of self-meditation each day to resonate with yourself, you can do things all day from a heightened state of abundance. But if you don't acknowledge and connect with yourself first, you can end up feeling resentful about the daily demands that omit you from the experience.

Seeing Through Projection

"We don't see the world as it is. We see it as we are."

—Paul Gonyea

One of the greatest benefits of Mirror Work is that it changes what is reflected back to you. Whatever personal biases you hold for yourself will surely be reflected in your everyday experiences. If you believe that you are unworthy, your life experiences will mirror your truth back to you.

I Grant You Permission to Love Yourself

I believe that self-love is the journey every soul on earth is incarnated to learn and, once we fully love ourselves, only then are we free to unconditionally love others.

This is because we are no longer loving others to be loved back. We are no longer expecting others to treat us a certain way in order to extend our love to them. We are simply loving for the sake of loving. No strings attached.

I have observed and experienced the power of

loving yourself will have on your life in its fullness. This includes the positive impact it has had in all my relationships, personally and professionally. And I am still being presented with opportunities for even deeper uncovering and understanding of the power of self-love. Sometimes I find it hard to believe that so many years of my life were consumed with seeking love and approval from others. I have set myself free.

Have you ever experienced self-love in such a way that you were blissfully in love with being unapologetically you? Free without the worry of how others might perceive you? I hope so, but if not and just in case you need it, I grant you permission to *love yourself unconditionally.* Today and every day!

Truth Be Told

Since you are love and it is your true nature, then you don't need to *learn* self-love; you simply need to awaken to the truth of who you really are. You can never be truly happy and content until you do. Let go of your judgments toward yourself. Your true essence is Love. You are a divine spark of love and light no matter what you have been told.

Truth be told, no one outside yourself has the power to influence your feelings inside yourself without your permission. To love ourselves is to remember we don't have to do anything to experience the love we already are. Be still and know that you are love.

And, the only commitment that counts is the one you keep with yourself. Make a commitment to yourself to nurture an unconditional loving relationship with the most important person you will ever meet, YOU. Love yourself deliberately and on purpose. Love yourself unconditionally because you are beautiful and worthy of love.

From this day forward, I encourage you to take five or ten minutes for yourself each day to connect with the wonderful, beautiful person looking back at you in the mirror. Just sit and be. Appreciate yourself for simply being you. Realize if you don't take wonderful care of the person you are looking at, who will?

There is no finish line, so I encourage you to:
- Tell yourself, "I love you" and personalize it by using your name.
- Ask yourself, "What can I do to make me feel happy today?"

Thank you for allowing me to be part of your self-love journey. Please know that I love you and I invite you to reach out if you want to take a deeper dive. I offer coaching, workshops, training and speeches to help individuals and groups experience their spiritual magnificence. And always remember that you are precious and free.

Thank you for taking this journey with me. Love Always. Namaste.

Happy Mirroring,
Coach Greta

About the Author

Greta Counts, affectionately known as "Coach Greta," is a born leader, gifted teacher, and inspiring friend. She has an absolute passion for developing people to their personal and professional greatness. Greta believes that all people are divinely creative beings with unlimited potential.

She is the founder and CEO of the Center for Self-Awareness, a company that offers transformational principles and practices to inspire people to recognize their magnificence, deeply connect with their divine selves and expand their consciousness.

She received her degree in Business Administration from Georgia State University with a concentration in Organizational Theory and Behavior. She is a Licensed Practitioner in Metaphysics with the Centers for Spiritual Living and Emerson Institute. She is a Hay House accredited Heal Your Life © Licensed Workshop Facilitator and Certified Life Coach. She is also a Spiritual Leader with Unity Worldwide Ministries and an ordained minister and transformational speaker. She has been in the personal growth and professional development industry for more than 22 years.

Greta is the proud mother of beautiful adult twin daughters and enjoys roller-skating, waterfall hiking, salsa dancing, and painting.

Visit her website at
www.CenterforSelfAwareness.com.